SAINT DOMINIC SAVIO

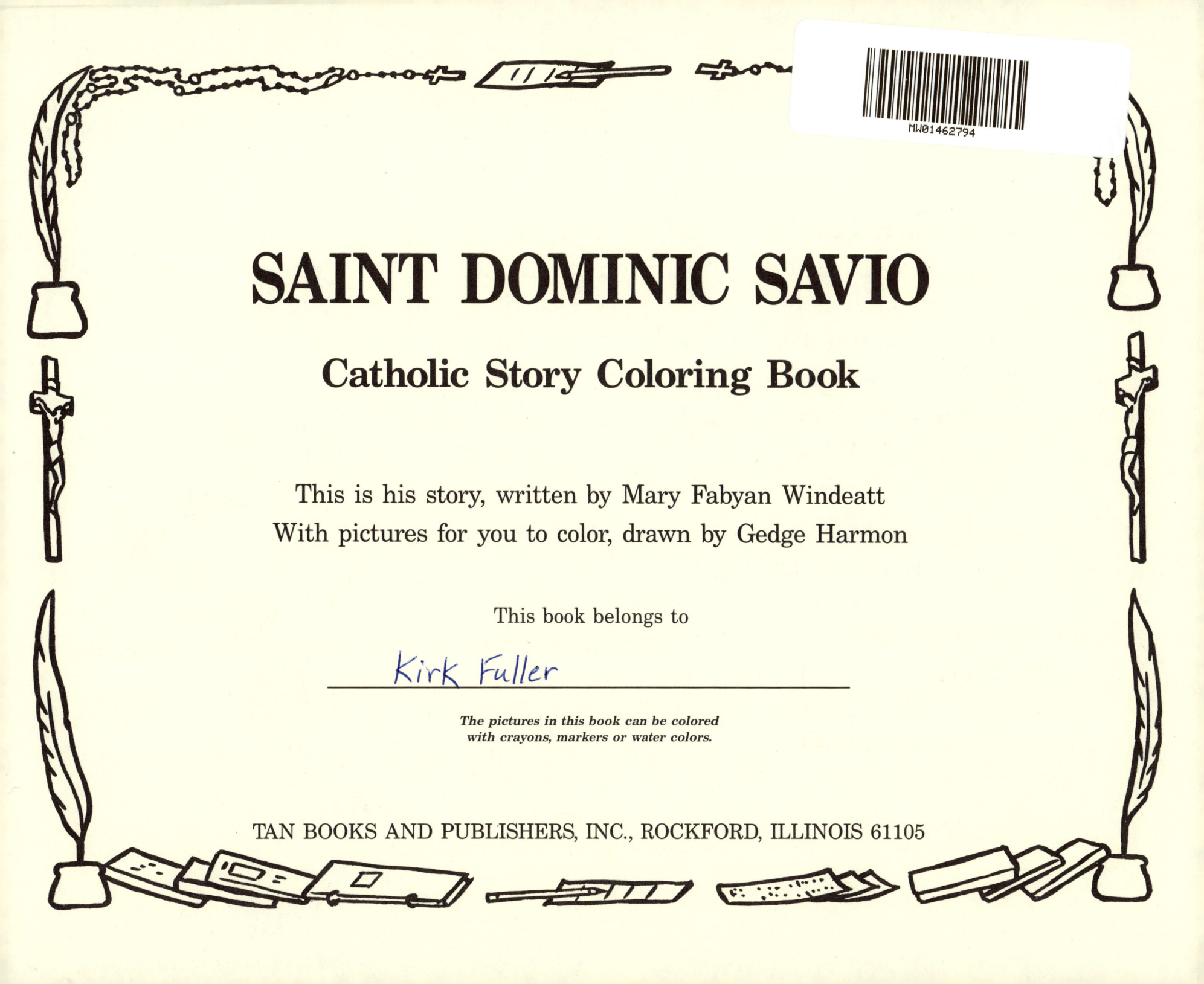

Catholic Story Coloring Book

This is his story, written by Mary Fabyan Windeatt
With pictures for you to color, drawn by Gedge Harmon

This book belongs to

Kirk Fuller

*The pictures in this book can be colored
with crayons, markers or water colors.*

TAN BOOKS AND PUBLISHERS, INC., ROCKFORD, ILLINOIS 61105

CHAPTER ONE

CHARLES SAVIO, the blacksmith of Murialdo, paused briefly at his task of shoeing the miller's horse. Winter was a bleak time in northern Italy, with many a sharp wind sweeping down from the mountains to chill a man's bones. Now, though, on this November afternoon of the year 1847....

"It's a really bad day," he told himself. "The snow's getting deeper all the time." But even as he toyed with the idea of closing up shop and going home early, a breathless five-year-old boy burst through the door.

"Oh, Daddy! Daddy! Guess what?"

Smiling, Charles reached down for the rosy-cheeked little figure and swung him to his shoulder. "Well, now, Dominic! Is it good news or bad?"

"Oh, good news, Daddy! Very good news!"

"Very good news, eh? Well, let me think—"

Eyes sparkling, Dominic waited eagerly for his father to speak. But after a moment, unable to contain his excitement any longer—

"Oh, Daddy, you'll never guess right in a million years! I'm to serve Mass tomorrow all by myself! Isn't that wonderful?"

Charles' lips twitched with amusement. "All by yourself, son, when you're only five years old? Come, now—there must be a mistake of some sort...."

But Dominic's eyes continued to shine. "Oh, no, Daddy! Father John told me so himself just a little while ago."

SAINT DOMINIC SAVIO

Page Three

CHAPTER TWO

THAT night there was considerable excitement in the Savio home. Even three-year-old Raimonda sensed that her brother had suddenly taken on new importance. However, when both children were in bed, Bridget Savio looked anxiously at her husband. "It's going to be dreadfully cold for Dominic to be up for Father John's Mass," she said slowly. "And dark, too. What about it, Charles? Don't you think we should send word for an older boy to serve?"

Charles grinned. "And break our little lad's heart? No, Bridget, let him go."

So at five o'clock the next morning, as he had hoped and planned, Dominic served Mass all by himself in the icy little church of Murialdo. All went well, too—at least until it came time to move the Missal from the right side of the altar to the left (so that the priest might read the Gospel according to custom). Then the awkward burden of book and stand proved too much for the small boy, and he tumbled headlong down the steps.

Father John held his breath when he heard the bumps. Dear God, was the lad hurt? But a hasty glance assured him that all was well. The five-year-old struggled to his feet at once and started up again with book and stand.

"The Lord be with you," said the priest, his eyes twinkling in spite of himself.

"And . . . and with thy spirit!" panted Dominic triumphantly.

SAINT DOMINIC SAVIO

Page Five

CHAPTER THREE

WHEN he returned home from Mass, Dominic was not much concerned about his accident. "I'll be more careful next time," he told his mother cheerfully. "All that matters is that I said 'thank You' to God this morning."

Bridget stared. "You said 'thank You' to God? Why, what do you mean?"

"I heard Mass, Mama. Isn't that the best way to thank God for all the nice things He does for us?"

"Of course, dear. But who ever told you that?"

"Nobody. I just thought of it myself. You see, I want to thank God all I can. He likes it, Mama."

Bridget often pondered her boy's words. Dominic might be only five, but he surely said the most surprising things. Wise things, too, far beyond his years. However, one night she was ashamed of the child's behavior. A certain Joseph Bianchi had come for supper and Dominic had left the table at the very beginning of the meal without a word of excuse. Thus, when the visitor had departed—

"Dominic, what happened to you tonight?" she demanded indignantly. "Why were you so rude?"

Charles' eyes were grave. "Yes, son. Explain yourself."

Unabashed, the boy faced his parents. "That man didn't say grace before supper!" he burst out. "He didn't thank God for any of the nice food! Oh, Mama! Daddy! I just couldn't watch him eating like . . . like an animal!"

SAINT DOMINIC SAVIO

Page Seven

CHAPTER FOUR

THE parents glanced uneasily at each other. Yes, Joseph Bianchi had seemed to down his food without a thought of God. But did a mere child have the right to rebuke an older person's bad manners, especially when that person was the family's guest? Surely not! Yet when the problem was presented to Father John, the priest only smiled. "Don't worry," he said. "One of these days Dominic and I will have a little talk about charity."

When the pastor had explained to him about charity, Dominic hung his head. How thoughtless he had been the other night! How much better to have stayed quietly at table while Mama or Daddy handled the matter of saying grace before meals....

"Well, I'm glad you understand, Dominic," said Father John, smiling. "After all, the practice of charity is the surest way to heaven. And you do want to go there, don't you?"

The little boy's face brightened. "Oh, yes, Father!"

"Then ask Our Lady to help you to know and love the virtue of charity: to act as Jesus acted when He was your age."

"You mean be good without letting on about it, Father? Without hurting people's feelings like... like I did the other night?"

The priest's eyes twinkled. "That's one way, son. But remember this: the more you think about charity, the more ways you'll find to put it into practice."

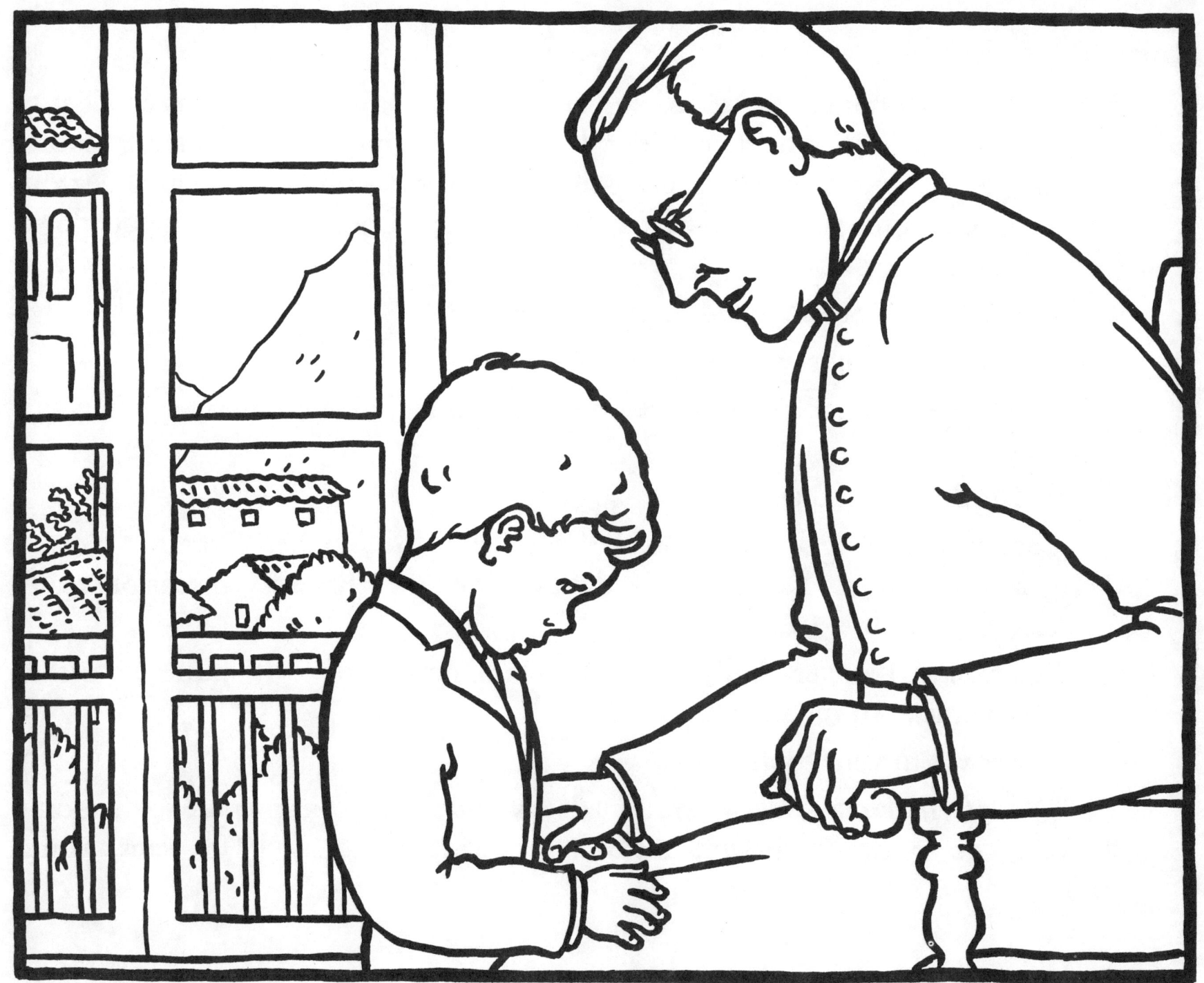

SAINT DOMINIC SAVIO

Page Nine

CHAPTER FIVE

BY the time Dominic was seven, he had made a surprising discovery. Charity was not just a matter of being polite or kind, even of giving food, money or clothes to poor people. It also meant being good to one's own soul by keeping it free from sin. Thus, on Easter Sunday, 1849, the day of his First Communion, he wrote down four important resolutions:

1. I will keep Sundays and Holy Days holy.

2. My best friends will be Jesus and Mary.

3. I will go to confession more often, and to Holy Communion as often as I am allowed.

4. Death, rather than sin.

Charles and Bridget Savio scarcely knew what to say when Dominic showed them his resolutions. Death, rather than sin! Did their little seven-year-old really understand what this meant?

"Of course I understand!" burst out Dominic eagerly. "It means I'd rather die than be mean to my soul."

"Be mean to your soul!"

"Yes. Oh, Mama! Daddy! God made my soul to be clean and pure so that some day it can go to heaven. It wouldn't be a bit charitable to spoil His plans, would it?"

SAINT DOMINIC SAVIO

Page Eleven

CHAPTER SIX

AT the age of nine, when he had finished the regular course of studies in the village school of Murialdo, Dominic became a student at Castelnuovo, three miles away. This meant a daily walk of twelve miles for the boy, since he always came home at noon to help with the chores.

"It's too much for you, lad," declared a neighboring farmer one day. "Why wear yourself out with more schooling when you already know how to read and write?"

Dominic laughed. "I don't mind it, sir. Besides, I've got to know a lot if I'm going to be a priest."

"A priest! And who's going to pay for you at the Seminary?"

"I don't know, sir, but God does. He'll see to things."

Yes, Dominic's heart was now set on saying "thank You" to God by offering himself for service in the priesthood. However, this did not keep him from enjoying life with other boys his age. There were games at school, also at home when chores were finished. Thus, one day in the summer of 1852, when Dominic was ten, he went with some friends to a shallow pond not far from home. None of the group could swim, but it would be fun enough just to splash around in the cool water.

"Come on, let's play at something," suggested one lad presently.

Dominic's eyes shone. "Leapfrog!" he shouted. "Line up, everybody! I'll go first. . . ."

SAINT DOMINIC SAVIO

Page Thirteen

CHAPTER SEVEN

THE leapfrog game was great fun, and Dominic thoroughly enjoyed it. It was also fun to duck an unsuspecting neighbor who was trying to float on his back, then be ducked in turn. After a while, though, Dominic noticed that while he was busy trying to master a few real swimming strokes, several of his friends had withdrawn into a tight little circle. Now they were snickering among themselves.

"Ha, ha, Tony! That's a good one!"

"Yes, but wait'll you hear this...."

As it suddenly dawned on him what was happening—that one of his friends was telling a bad story—Dominic's cheeks flamed. How could anyone bear to listen to such filth? And having splashed quickly to shore, he picked up his clothes and began to dress.

"Heh, what's the matter?" cried one of the boys. "It's not time to go home yet."

The ten-year-old scowled. "I know. But I don't like bad talk."

"Bad talk, eh? Well, well! Just listen to the little sissy!"

"Ha, ha! So Mama's baby doesn't think we're good enough for him?"

Dominic's lips quivered. It wasn't easy to be made fun of, to leave the pond when he had been having such fun. But wasn't "death, rather than sin" one of the resolutions he had made at First Communion time? Well, here was the chance to prove he still meant that holy promise to God.

SAINT DOMINIC SAVIO

Page Fifteen

CHAPTER EIGHT

IN October of that same year, 1852, the Savio family moved from Murialdo to Mondonio, the small town where Charles Savio had been born. The pastor here, Father Cugliero, was also the schoolmaster, and before long Dominic and he had become good friends. One day, as the two were out walking together—

"So you'd like to be a priest, eh, lad?"

"Oh, yes, Father!"

"Well, we'll ask Father John Bosco's advice the next time he's in the neighborhood. Of course you've heard of him?"

The boy nodded eagerly. Who hadn't heard of this great priest? Why, rumor had it that he was a saint who could actually read a person's soul! That the Oratory of Saint Francis de Sales, the school for poor boys which he had founded in Turin, was one of the city's marvels....

"Oh, yes, Father, I've heard of Father Bosco. But will he really be around here some day?"

"Of course, since he likes to visit his family at Becchi, only a couple of miles away. The next time he's home, I'll arrange for you to see him."

That night Dominic found it hard to go to sleep. What would it be like to meet a saint? To hear him speak? Perhaps—oh, great joy—even to receive his blessing?

SAINT DOMINIC SAVIO   **Page Seventeen**

CHAPTER NINE

ON October 2, 1854, Dominic knew the answer to all three questions. Even more. He found himself in Becchi, with Father Bosco agreeing to accept him as a student at the Oratory, his famous school for boys in Turin.

"Oh, Father, how can I ever thank you?" he burst out.

The priest, a sturdily built man of thirty-nine, clapped Dominic on the back. "Doing what you're told would be the best way," he said, his eyes twinkling. "Do you think you can manage that, son?"

Dominic grinned. What a wonderful man Father Bosco was! So friendly and full of fun! Why, he didn't begin to resemble the pale and rather serious character which he, Dominic, had decided a saint must be—

"I'll try, Father. I'll do my very best."

"That's fine, young fellow. You see, I think there's good material in you."

"Good material! Why, what do you mean, Father?"

"What do you think I mean?"

"Well, that I'm like cloth, maybe?"

"Exactly. A fine cloth that Jesus wants to have made into a garment for Himself. Now, how about it? Will you let me be the tailor?"

Twelve-year-old Dominic nodded eagerly. "Oh, yes, Father! Of course!"

SAINT DOMINIC SAVIO

Page Nineteen

CHAPTER TEN

A FEW days later, when he arrived in the great city of Turin, Dominic was beside himself with amazement. Never before had he seen so many people, or such huge churches and public buildings. As for the Oratory—well, it was certainly the most surprising kind of school. About ninety boys were enrolled here—some from wealthy homes, others from the slums. Studies were of all kinds, too: for those who wanted a regular education, as well as for those who preferred to learn a trade.

"Don't be surprised at anything you see around here," warned Michael Rua, one of the older boys, as he took Dominic for a walk about the rather untidy grounds. "The Oratory's the only school of its kind in Italy—an experiment in Christian living. You'll find we have some rather bad characters, as well as some very good ones."

Dominic's eyes widened. "Bad characters?"

"Yes, boys from broken homes who'd never have the chance to amount to anything except for Father Bosco's kindness. But he has faith in every one of them, even the worst."

Soon Dominic realized the truth in Michael's words. Yes, the Oratory school was an experiment, supported by the faith, hope and charity of Father Bosco and his numerous friends. And though the experiment was scarcely twelve years old, already it had helped many a boy to know, love and serve God with his whole heart.

SAINT DOMINIC SAVIO

Page Twenty-One

CHAPTER ELEVEN

DOMINIC was extremely happy at the Oratory. However, in April, 1855, shortly after his thirteenth birthday, he began to worry. Was it right to be so full of joy? he asked himself. To look forward to recreation time with so much eagerness? True, in a recent sermon Father Bosco had insisted that everyone could be a saint, easily and simply, by using the grace God gave him. Yet hadn't he, Dominic, read of certain monks and hermits—now great saints—who had kept perpetual silence, wept constantly over their sins and fasted for long periods on bread and water? Ah, yes—being a saint must be a difficult business after all....

Soon Dominic was on the verge of despair at what he considered to be his lack of spiritual progress. How hard to turn away from innocent pleasures! How impossible to please God as the monks and hermits had done!

"Nonsense, boy!" exclaimed Father Bosco, when he finally discovered the reason for his young friend's low spirits. "Don't you know God gives different graces to different people? Right now, for instance, He's giving you the chance to be a schoolboy saint—no more, no less."

Dominic stared. "A schoolboy saint, Father! But I thought—"

"Never mind what you thought. Just now I see a ball game starting in the far field. Hurry over there and get in on it, will you? And enjoy yourself, lad—the way the Child Jesus did when He played games with His friends!"

SAINT DOMINIC SAVIO

Page Twenty-Three

CHAPTER TWELVE

SOON Dominic was happier than he had ever been in his whole life. A boy his age could earn sainthood merely by doing little things well—like studying and running errands? Even eating, sleeping and playing games? How wonderful!

"It was the Devil who made me think I had to act like a monk or hermit in order to please God," he decided finally. "He knew that I'd soon grow discouraged and stop trying to be good. But now—oh, how different everything is!"

Yes, the knowledge that he was meant to be a schoolboy saint—no more, no less—opened up a whole new world to Dominic. To the best of his ability he now set himself to doing everyday duties well, and to getting his friends to do the same. After all, long prayers and difficult penances weren't what God wanted of boys in school. Short prayers, well said, Mass and Holy Communion whenever possible, were far more to the point. And charity, of course. Charity of all kinds.

One day Dominic chanced upon an unusual way of practicing charity. Two friends had had a serious quarrel, and now were about to engage in a duel with stones. "No, no!" he cried. "You'll get hurt . . . maybe even killed!"

The enemies glared. "Beat it, Dominic! This isn't any affair of yours."

But the boy held his ground. "I won't beat it," he said quietly, pulling a crucifix from his pocket and stepping quickly between the pair. "If you must fight, throw the stones at me—or at Him!"

SAINT DOMINIC SAVIO

Page Twenty-Five

CHAPTER THIRTEEN

THE boys gasped as Dominic raised his crucifix aloft, but he paid them no heed. "Go ahead," he insisted. "Just say to yourself: 'Christ died innocent and pardoned His enemies, but I want my revenge.'"

However, as neither horrified lad made a move, Dominic's eyes gradually softened. "Oh, come on, fellows!" he urged. "If you can't throw a stone at a little wooden crucifix, how can you bear to be mean to Jesus in your own souls? He's truly present there, you know—far more so than in this piece of wood. Now, how about shaking hands and making up?"

"But . . . but he insulted my family!"

"He . . . he called me names!"

"So what? Jesus was insulted lots of times by the Romans and the Jews. And called names, too. But did He hold a grudge? Or His Blessed Mother?"

"That's different."

"Of course it's different! Jesus was God, and He could have wiped out His enemies with a single glance. But He didn't because He wanted to show the rest of us how to act. Come on, can't you say 'thank You' for all that He put up with for our sakes?"

For a moment there was silence. Then, slowly, the former enemies shuffled awkwardly toward each other. "I . . . I'm sorry," muttered one.

"It . . . it's all right," grunted the other.

SAINT DOMINIC SAVIO

Page Twenty-Seven

CHAPTER FOURTEEN

BY the spring of 1856, when Dominic had been at the Oratory for some eighteen months, Father Bosco suddenly realized that the boy's health was beginning to fail. "You've been working too hard," he said reproachfully. "Why didn't you tell me you weren't feeling well?"

The fourteen-year-old boy managed a reassuring smile. "I'm all right, Father. But please, the next time you go to Rome—"

"Yes, lad?"

"Tell Pope Pius the Ninth to keep on working for the conversion of England. God is preparing a great triumph for the Church there."

"W-what?"

Dominic nodded eagerly. "Yes, Father, I know it sounds strange, but after I received Holy Communion this morning I saw a vast plain covered by thousands of people groping about under a dark cloud. Suddenly a beam of light pierced the cloud, and Pope Pius the Ninth came walking across the plain with a torch in his hand. Then a voice said to me: 'This is England. The torch is the light of faith which is to illumine England.' Then the cloud vanished, it became bright as noon, and all the people began to rejoice because now they could see where they were going."

Father Bosco stared in amazement. Was young Dominic Savio actually so close to being a saint that God had allowed him to see into the future?

SAINT DOMINIC SAVIO

Page Twenty-Nine

CHAPTER FIFTEEN

BY the fall of that same year, 1856, Father Bosco was practically convinced that Dominic had arrived at the state of heroic sanctity. This in itself was sufficient reason to rejoice, but when he considered that the boy had reached this goal merely by doing little things well, his heart sang. What good this youngster would accomplish once he entered God's service! Why, some day he might even go to England and help in that country's conversion. . . .

"Death, rather than sin," mused the priest. "Well, wherever he goes, I know Dominic will get the little ones to make his motto their own."

Some months later, however, Dominic's schooling had to be interrupted. A change of air was absolutely necessary for the boy, declared Father Bosco, if he was to avoid a serious breakdown. Charles and Bridget Savio agreed, and so on March 1, 1857, Dominic returned home to Mondonio.

"Don't worry, dear," said Bridget soothingly. "We'll have you well in no time at all."

Charles nodded. "That's right, son. Fresh country air, your mother's good cooking, plenty of rest—why, you'll be a different boy in just a few days!"

Dominic blinked back the tears as he looked at his parents, twelve-year-old Raimonda and the seven other children whom God had sent the Savio family through the years. "No, no!" he choked. "Oh, Mama! Daddy! I . . . I've come home to die. . . ."

SAINT DOMINIC SAVIO

Page Thirty-One

CHAPTER SIXTEEN

CHARLES and Bridget looked at each other anxiously. Dominic wasn't well, of course, but surely there was no reason to believe—

"Son, you mustn't say such things!"

"Of course not. Father Bosco wouldn't like it."

A week later, however, when the boy had developed a bad case of pneumonia, the local pastor decided to bring him the Last Sacraments. "What did I tell you?" whispered Dominic, a faint smile on his lips. "I am going to die. But please don't feel bad, Mama. Or you either, Daddy. Oh, if you just knew how much I'll be able to do for you in heaven...."

Yet on the evening of the next day, March 9, 1857, Charles and Bridget broke down completely. Their little son was dead—twenty-four days short of his fifteenth birthday! And he had wanted so much to be a priest....

"Don't grieve," wrote Father Bosco from Turin. "God has great plans for Dominic."

But it was not until June 12, 1954, that the truth of these words was fully realized. Then, at a splendid ceremony in Saint Peter's Basilica in Rome, Pope Pius the Twelfth solemnly declared Dominic Savio to be a canonized saint of the Church. Even more. If boys and girls would make his motto their own, he said—death, rather than sin—Dominic would surely help them to be saints, too.